United Kingdom Readi

Minibook Series No 7

Phonological Awareness Classroom Strategies

Frances James

Minibook Series

Series Editor: Alison B. Littlefair

Already Published

Genres in the Classroom	Alison B. Littlefair
Running Family Reading Groups	Sue Beverton, Ann Stuart, Morag Hunter-Carsch, Cecilia Oberist
Miscue Analysis in the Classroom	Robin Campbell
Teaching Hand Writing	Peter Smith
Teaching Spelling	Brigid Smith
Supporting Struggling Readers	Diana Bentley and Dee Reid

Issue No. 7:   **Phonological Awareness: Classroom Strategies**
Issue Author: Frances James

ISBN   1 897638 07 8
ISSN   1350 - 7664

Published by: United Kingdom Reading Association
Unit 2, Station Road, Shepreth, Nr Royston, Herts.
SG8 6PZ, UK

March 1996

A Catalogue record for this book is available from the British Library

CONTENTS

Introduction	5
Research background	5
Early development	7
Rhyming	12
Appreciation of alliteration	16
Linking children's oral knowledge with print	17
Onset and rime	19
Reinforcing children's sense of analogy	20
Using phonemes	22
Assessment	23
Conclusion	25
References	27

INTRODUCTION

As a teacher I always found the teaching of phonics one of the greatest challenges. It seemed a dry and, in many cases, a meaningless activity. My lack of enthusiasm, I am sure, was transmitted to the children. I religiously went through the initial sounds but when faced with the vowels and more sophisticated sound-letter relationships I hoped that the children would just intuitively "pick them up".

"Phonics" are, however, unavoidable. To become fluent accurate readers children need to develop specific skills and concepts and to acquire specific knowledge. They need to develop a sight vocabulary, using their visual memory skills; they need to understand about the whole process of reading and to use their understanding of language to make sense of what they have read. They need to use their detailed knowledge of spoken language - the sounds and rhythm of, and within, words, and relate this to the written representation of words. This latter skill is traditionally known as "phonics".

Teaching phonics has tended to concentrate on the initial sounds of words - just as I did. I did not recognise that children required an appreciation of the sound qualities of whole words before tackling individual sounds nor how they then needed to build on the knowledge of initial sounds to develop their spelling or to help them read unknown words. This broader approach to teaching the relationship between letters (and letter strings) to sounds, necessary for reading, has resulted largely from a growing bank of research evidence. To reflect this breadth of approach it is more properly regarded as developing children's phonological awareness rather than "teaching phonics".

RESEARCH BACKGROUND

Phonological Awareness

Phonology refers to the sound system of a language. Children, from the youngest age, will be developing an appreciation of the qualities of sounds of words. Young babies play with sound, repeating specific syllables and responding to familiar repetitive rhythmic phrases or jingles. The phonological skills required to be a fluent accurate reader are sophisticated but the recent research into phonological awareness provides teachers with a way of approaching the task, of developing these skills, which builds on the children's existing knowledge, places the skills in context and allows the activities to be enjoyable for the teacher and the children. It recognises the importance of children's early language experiences (especially with rhymes, poems and stories) in the development of phonic knowledge. The emphasis is upon phonological awareness and how the child uses this awareness to recognise and develop analogies, through their experience with print.

Bryant and Bradley (1985) identified the importance of early oral experiences, particularly in relationship to nursery rhyme and this work has been taken forward by Goswami and Bryant (1990) and Goswami (1994) to look at the importance of analogy (the shared spelling patterns of many words that rhyme) in children's reading development.

These researchers, and others, focus on the different phonological elements in words. The largest is the syllable. Syllables can be broken down into onsets and rimes - the rime is the part that allows the syllable to rhyme with others and the onset the initial sounds. The phonemes are the smallest units of sound that can change the meaning of a word.

The following table shows how words can be broken down into different phonological elements.

Word	Syllable	Onset	Rime	Phonemes
dog	dog	d	og	d-o-g
stroke	stroke	`str	oke	s-t-r-o-k-e
chick	chick	ch	ick	ch-i-c-k
duckling	duck	d	uck	d-u-c-k
	ling	l	ing	l-i-n-g

From this table one can see that in the word "dog" there is one syllable but that this syllable can be separated into an onset "d" and rime "og". The rime is found in words that rhyme with "dog" - for example, "fog, log, frog". The onsets in those words are "f", "l" and "fr" respectively. The smallest units of sound (the phonemes) will change the meaning of the word. For example, changing the phoneme "o" to "i" makes the word "dig" and changing the phoneme "g" to "t" will make the word "dot". These kinds of manipulations can be made with the syllables in words of more than one syllable, as in "duck/ling".

Developing Essential Skills

The skills, in this book, are presented in a broadly developmental order. As with all teaching activities it will be necessary to differentiate the skills and concepts. Some children will arrive in school with a good knowledge of nursery rhymes and be able to match words that rhyme with great ease. They may have played plenty of games, such as "I Spy" with families and friends. These children will already be developing a good sense of phonology and they will need different activities from other children who have poorly developed general listening skills and possibly are unable to distinguish individual words in speech. However, because so many of the activities are fun, and will consolidate important skills, many can be used with the class as a whole and you can plan specific activities for smaller groups of children when you wish to address particular skills.

EARLY DEVELOPMENT

LISTENING SKILLS

If children are to develop an accurate appreciation of the sounds in words they need to have sophisticated listening skills. Many teachers have observed that children appear to have poorer listening skills than in the past. It is difficult to substantiate this observation but it is undoubtedly true that the world in which we live relies very heavily on visual information - it is possible to follow a story on television through the visual cues paying only scant attention to the oral information. Oral traditions do not seem to have such a place in modern culture.

Infant teachers have always placed considerable importance on developing children's listening skills through a range of activities.

Story-telling

In her book "Beginning to Read" Marylin Jaguar Adams (1991) identifies the impact that children's exposure to stories can have on their later reading ability. She quotes a study in which a group of parents received some training on how to share stories with their children and the positive impact that this approach had on the children's vocabulary. The training emphasised the interactive approach to story-telling, involving the children as active participants in the process.

There are certain features of this approach.

- talking about the book before it is read - predicting the story from the pictures etc.

- asking the child open-ended questions (questions that demand more than a yes/no answer) as the story is read

- actively seeking the child's opinion about the book - the characters, the course that the plot is taking, what might have happened etc., what aspects of the book they enjoyed

- encouraging the child to join in.

Some children, when they arrive at school, have not had the benefit of a rich language and literary environment and so it falls to the teachers to provide such opportunities. This is difficult in a busy classroom and so some schools have enlisted the help of volunteers to tell stories to small groups of children or even to individual children.

Many schools encourage parent helpers to come into the school. These helpers are frequently asked to hear children read; this, undoubtedly, provides invaluable practice for the children. For some children, though, it is more appropriate for them to hear stories to help them develop listening and other language skills. If schools are unable to recruit sufficient help from the parent body they can look at establishing links with the community, for example, the University of the Third Age or the Women's Institute. Local Community Education services are often able to provide information about groups who may be interested in working with schools.

Providing training for the volunteers is important; some schools have produced excellent materials to support this training. Most volunteers are more confident when telling stories from books but they can be encouraged to include rhymes and poems in their repertoire. If you are truly fortunate, you may chance on a volunteer who tells stories from their own past or imagination.

The training should include an explanation about why it is important that children are exposed to a wide variety of literary and language experiences. If possible arrange for a display of high quality children's literature including poetry as well fiction and non-fiction. There should be a description of the major features of the approach, with examples of open-ended questions. One of the most effective ways of training is by modelling the techniques. The emphasis of all the training is that the time spent with the child should be a pleasurable experience.

Listening Games

There are many games that can be played to encourage listening.

- "Chinese Whispers" - sit the children in a semi circle. Whisper a short message to the first child. The child whispers what they have heard to their neighbour and so the message is passed to the end of the line. The last child announces what they heard to the whole group. Any differences from the original message are noted. If the message has changed, the children report what they heard to find out how it changed in its passage around the group.

- "Simon Says" - The teacher or a nominated child gives instructions to the group. If they preface the instruction with "Simon Says" then others have to complete the action. When "Simon Says" is not said then they do not. Children who do not note the difference are "out".

- "Kim's Game" (a listening version). Play 4 (or more) different instruments behind a screen. Repeat the sequence but omit 1 sound. Ask the children to identify which one was omitted.

Listening Activities in the classroom

It is important to encourage the children to become aware of the sounds in their environment.

- Gather a group together and ask them to listen carefully to all the sounds that they can hear and to identify the source. They can record what they hear pictorially.

- Broaden this activity to the wider environment - ask them what they hear as they walk to school, as they lie in bed etc.

- Arrange a screen in the classroom. Provide a range of objects that make a noise behind the screen. Let the children take it in turns to go behind the screen and choose an object for the other children to identify.

There are many commercially produced materials which can encourage listening skills, including reproductions of environmental sounds and animal sounds.

Following Instructions

This is, obviously, an essential part of school life. Note those children who have difficulty remembering instructions which have a number of elements - this may be indicative of poor listening or memory skills. (An example of an instruction with one element is "stand still", with two elements "stand still, lift your foot" and three elements "stand still, lift your foot and raise your hand".) Use PE, drama and other activities to develop their ability to follow gradually more complex instructions. Ask children to repeat your instructions, this will enable the child to rehearse the phrase and will also allow you to assess the child's accuracy.

Listening to Words

Words in speech can seem like one continuous flow of sound. The delineation between separate words is not clear, there are no obvious conventions, such as the spaces between words in print. This can contribute to some children having difficulty in establishing a one-to-one correspondence between spoken words and print.

- Encourage the children to listen carefully to themselves and others.

- Ask the children to count the number of words as you say short phrases.

- Write the words on cards (or use "Breakthrough to Literacy") to emphasise the number and separateness of words.

Children also need to appreciate that what they hear is reflected in print.

- Write some long words (caterpillar, telephone, motorway) and some short words (it, am, he) on individual cards. Choose one card from each set. Show them to the children and say one of the words. Ask the children which one they think it is. The aim of this activity is to make the link between the length of the sound of the word and its print representation.
(Use long words to encourage children to listen for smaller words within them.)

Awareness of Rhythm

Children need to be able to recognise the rhythm within words. This will allow them to identify syllables - an essential skill, and the more sophisticated phonological elements; onset, rime and phonemes. To be able to break words up into syllables is an important strategy when attempting to spell an unknown word or to learn to say a new word. Anyone learning a foreign language will recognise how they break up new words into manageable chunks, in other words, syllables, to help them to remember. Developing the children's appreciation of rhythm may be undertaken through a number of language and music activities.

- Share stories, rhymes and poems with a strong rhythmical structure, encouraging the children to join in. "The Three Little Pigs" is a good example as children enjoy reciting the wolf's refrain - "Then I'll huff and I'll puff and I'll blow your house down". Other examples include "The Billy Goats Gruff" - all the goats go "trip, trap, trip, trap, over the rickety bridge", "The Ginger bread Man" - "Run, run as fast as you can. You can't catch me. I'm the Gingerbread Man".

- Provide the children with instruments to accompany the words.

- Teach the children action and marching rhymes; for example, "The Grand Old Duke of York", "Jelly on the Plate", "The Bear went over the Mountain".

- Clap out the rhythm of the children's names. These can be used to compose short musical pieces.

- Allow the children to experience music with a variety of rhythms - dance music from around the world is a great source of different rhythms, which the children enjoy moving to and accompanying. Choose music from South America, Africa and the Caribbean which use strong drum rhythms. Flamenco music frequently has complex accompanying clapping rhythms.

- Extend the range of musical instruments in the school by making instruments with the children.

- Build on the work on the rhythm of words to teach the children to recognise words of different syllabic lengths. Clap the syllables with the children. Sort words into sets depending on the number of syllables that they contain.

- As the children become more familiar with print, write out words in big letters and let the children colour the syllables in different colours. Cut up words on their syllabic boundaries so that the children can make word jigsaws.

hippopotamus

RHYMING

Nursery Rhymes

Bryant and Bradley noted in their book "Children's Reading Difficulties" (1985) the importance of children's knowledge of nursery rhymes and their developing skills as readers. Nursery rhymes are, undoubtedly, a vast resource for introducing children to phonological features of words. It is vital that they have a central place in the early years classroom.

- Teach the children rhymes from our rich heritage of nursery rhymes. Use the numerous collections and analogies of nursery rhymes to extend the children's repertoire. Nursery rhymes can be linked to current topics within the classroom - for example if the class topic is "Food" teach the children rhymes such as "Half a Pound of Tuppenny rice", "Pease Porridge Hot", "Georgie Pogie, Pudding and Pie", "Simple Simon", "Little Jack Horner", "Little Miss Muffett", "Hot Cross Buns" and "Sing a Song of Sixpence".

- Let the children say them as a group or individually - be aware that some children may not be saying them accurately but just mouthing them at the back of the group.

- Say the rhymes with the children but miss out the rhyming word for the children to "fill in". This will begin to heighten the children's sensitivity to rhyme.

- Use a tape recorder for the children to make a collection of favourite class rhymes. These can be illustrated in a big class book - many of the rhymes lend themselves to exciting classroom display.

- Use the rhymes as an impetus for drama work or the use of puppets.

- Include other types of rhyme; for example, number clapping, nonsense and action rhymes. Number rhymes (for example "One, Two Three, Four, Five, Once I caught a fish alive", "Five Little Ducks went swimming one day" and "One, Two, Buckle my shoe") will reinforce the children's developing mathematical skills. Children respond well to nonsense rhymes - there are some very good contemporary collections, including those by Spike Milligan and Michael Rosen. Other collections, such as the work of Edward Lear introduce children to different rhyme forms - for example, limericks.

- Encourage children's knowledge, and use of playground rhymes. Many of these rhymes are accompanied by movements or are used by children to accompany skipping or clapping games or to determine who has the first "go" at something. Examples include "My boyfriend gave me an apple", "I went to a Chinese restaurant" "Ip, Dip", "One Potato, Two Potatoes". Many of these rhymes have distinct regional variations and Janet and Peter Opie(1969) included examples in their study of children's oral language.

- Involve other members of staff in promoting the children's use of the rhymes at play and lunch times. Remember to include the midday meal supervisors by asking them to join in with children's games at break times. Some schools have made booklets containing the most popular playground rhymes which can be shared with all members of staff, parents and children. The activities can have a very welcome side effect of improving playground behaviour - poor behaviour is often a result of the children not having anything purposeful to do. Games also teach children social skills such as turn taking and sharing.

- Many of the playground rhymes are regional and this allows schools to involve the community by asking local residents to record rhymes that they used to say when they were at school.

- Draw on the oral traditions of other cultural and ethnic groups represented in the community by asking members for children's rhymes that are part of their culture.

RHYMING WORDS

As the children become more and more familiar and confident with rhymes and poetry it is possible to draw their attention to the words that rhyme. This will begin to develop the children's appreciation of rimes. Eventually children will use this knowledge to build words using the beginning of the words - the onsets, and the endings - the rimes. (Rimes are the letter strings in words, or syllables, that allow them to rhyme with other words; for example *st***ick**; *h***ouse**; *f***all**)

All the work, at this stage, is done orally and so it is not necessary to discriminate between words that rhyme and share the same spelling pattern (tree - bee) and those that do not (tree - sea). One of the most important aspects of this work is to establish firmly the children's understanding of rhyme and to ensure that they use the word "rhyme" accurately.

Rhyming Sets

● Make collections of objects/pictures of words that rhyme. These could be "rhyming tables" or be used as sorting activities for the children.

● Use colours as a stimulus. Let the children draw things that rhyme with a given colour and stick their picture on the correct coloured paper.

● This activity may also be undertaken with numbers - let the children stick their pictures on large cut out numbers (a bun and sun on number 1 etc.)

● Use puppets, which have names with plenty of rhyming possibilities, to collect pictures of objects that rhyme with their names - e.g. Ann collects a can, fan, man, pan, van etc.

Rhyming Games

Many of the traditional word games can be adapted to focus on rhyming words.

● Play "I Spy" by saying "I spy with my little eye something that rhymes with.... hen" (answer - pen). As this is an oral activity it is not necessary that the words share the same spelling pattern you can include pairs like "bear - chair" and "Mabel - table"

● Link with the children's knowledge of nursery rhymes. Say well-known rhymes but change a key word and ask the children to complete the rhyme with an appropriate word. For example, "Jack and Jane, Went down the ......" (lane), or "Little Jack Moore, Sat on the ...." (floor). Let the children illustrate their new versions. If you write the words under the pictures try to include only those that share the same spelling pattern.

● Playing rhyming tag games such as "I packed my bag". Each of the subsequent objects have to rhyme with the first one. For example, "I packed my bag with a .....pin...tin...fin...bin...". The children have to remember all the previous contributions before they add a new word and so this may have a beneficial impact on their memory skills.

● Create riddles "I'm thinking of something that rhymes with....house" (mouse). On most occasions there will be more than one alternative. Encourage the children to think of as many as possible. If it is a large rhyming family, write the words down as the children say them and draw their attention to the spelling pattern.

● Gather together a collection of rhyming pictures with which one can play rhyming "Snap", "Pairs" and "Bingo"

APPRECIATION OF ALLITERATION

As the children begin to appreciate rhyme it is important that they should also be developing an appreciation of alliteration - words that begin with the same sounds. This will lead into work on onsets. (Onsets are the initial sounds of words and syllables; for example *st*ick; *h*ouse; *f*all)

Children enjoy playing with language and much of this work involves the children exploring sound qualities, within words, through play.

● Teach the children tongue twisters. Encourage them to say them as fast as they can. Use a tape recorder to record their efforts. Devise new tongue twisters using the children's own names as the stimulus.

● Let the children make up descriptive phrases about themselves, using adjectives which begin with the same sound; for example "Tim is tiny, trembling, terrified...". Write the completed phrases for the children. Let them highlight all the first letters that alliterate. Make a class book of all the children's names. Check that the children know the names of the letters and the sounds that they make.

● Make class alphabet book. You can choose the theme; for example, animals with an alliterative adjective. "An angry alligator, a busy bat, a careful cat, a dirty dog, an evil elephant etc."

● Collect objects/pictures that begin with the same sounds. Use these as a basis of a class or group collective story. All the objects have to be included in the story.

● Play tag word games which require the children to add adjectives which begin with the same sound - "The parson's cat is cool, cautious, canny, clever..." These may be collected into class big books or illustrated for a wall display.

● Provide the children with tiny stickers and ask them to place them on objects in the classroom which begin with a target sound.

● Ask the children to sort themselves into sets of children whose names begin with the same sound - get the children to record the results of this activity using sets or simple block graphs

● Remember current culture. Use the children's experience of advertising jingles which are alliterative. Invent slogans with the children for imaginary products - "Super Sita's silky saris".

LINKING CHILDREN'S ORAL KNOWLEDGE WITH PRINT

Alongside all the oral work that has been described above, the children will be being given considerable exposure to texts. From this they will be developing an appreciation of how print works (the directionality of print, the difference between words and letters etc.) and the beginnings of a small sight vocabulary. With such knowledge in place it is possible to begin to establish links between the children's oral knowledge and the characteristics of print. Specifically, words that begin with the same sound tend to begin with the same letter and those words that rhyme are likely to share a similar spelling pattern.

Many of the previous oral activities can be adapted to used with words. At this stage it is important that the words that you use **do** share the same spelling pattern. It is also important that child understand that letters have names and sounds - a common source of confusion for many children.

Rhyme

- Make collections of words that rhyme with the children. Write them down as families. Let the children illustrate them. Keep these as word lists for the children to use.

- Play matching games with cards that rhyme. Some children will need a picture cue to help them but others can begin to concentrate on the words.

- Play "Snap", "Bingo" and "Pairs". Again differentiate the materials that are used, recognising that some children will need the support of pictures.

- Ask the children to complete certain phrases that require rhymes: "A fox in a ....",(box), "A cat on the ..." (mat), "A frog on a ..."(log). Make these into a class book.

- Use the puppets to collect words that rhyme.

Seek every opportunity to draw the children's attention to the shared spelling pattern. Use a multi-sensory approach to reinforce the common letters; let them trace the words (cut out words using different textured materials: sand paper, shiny paper, corrugated paper etc.), write the words in sand, say the letter out loud and copywrite. Encourage the children to name the letters as they look carefully at the words.

Alliteration

Some initial sounds are more distinctive than others and there are some initial sounds that are easily confused (for example b and p.) The order that the sounds are introduced should take this into account.

- Cut out large letters and let the children find pictures from magazines to stick on the appropriate initial letter.

- Create an alphabet frieze with the children.

● Make a book of favourite tongue twisters. The children can highlight all the common initial sounds.

● Use the children's own names as a stimulus. Talk about initials. Let the children illustrate their own initials.

● Show children examples of old manuscripts, when the first letter of the page was richly illustrated. Use this as stimulus for a craft activity. Provide the children with glitter and sequins to make their letters as striking as possible.

● Children use the stickers with the appropriate letter written on to attach to objects which begin with a target sound.

ONSET AND RIME

When the children have a secure knowledge of rhyming words and initial sounds they can then use this knowledge to make words. This obviously has a direct impact on their spelling skills and will help them decode unknown words.

This is when the children begin to build words using their knowledge of rime (the part of the word or syllable that rhymes with other words) and onset (the initial sound) - for example, in the word "tall"; the onset is "t" and the rime "all".

● Provide the children with cards with a rime written on it and different onsets. Ask them to put the cards together to see what words they can make. For example, write "an" on a card and on other cards write the letters c, f, m, n, p, r and t. For some children you may wish to provide a word from the same family (in this example, "can") as a target word to help them make the rhyme connection. You can also provide pictures and the children have to match the words they make with the pictures.

● Make "flipper" books. The rime is clearly visible at the end of the book and there are different onsets on the proceeding pages. As the child turns the pages they record the words that they can see.

- Make two cardboard cubes. On one cube write a different onset on each face; on the other cube write different rimes on the faces. Children take turns to throw both cubes. If they can make a word from the onset and rime, that are shown on the two cubes, they score a point.

- Make dominoes which have a rime on the left-hand side and an onset on the right-hand side.

- Use concept keyboards. Devise overlays with onsets and rimes for the children to make words with.

REINFORCING CHILDREN'S SENSE OF ANALOGY

Analogy is the skill that allows one to draw on your previous knowledge to work out apparently new examples. This skill is central to all learning but its importance in developing reading has only recently been recognised through the work of Usha Goswami. In her work she has shown that if children are taught a target word such as "beak" many will then be able to use this knowledge to read a word like "peak". The children have a greater success rate reading the words that rhyme with the target word than other words, even if they share the same number of letters. Therefore if the target word is "beak" they will have more success reading "peak" than "bean".

If children have developed a sense of analogy through all the phonological work they will be able to draw on this knowledge to spell words (for example - "I need to spell 'mouse'. 'Mouse' rhymes with 'house'. I know how to spell 'house'. If I take away the initial sound of 'house' (h) and put in its place the first sound (m), I can spell 'mouse' "). Goswami has conducted a series of experiments to show that children do, indeed, use analogy to read unfamiliar words.

One of the ways that I have found most effective for introducing analogy is based on a strategy developed by Dr Peter Bryant and Dr Lynette Bradley. In their book "Children's Reading Difficulties" Bryant and Bradley (1985) described a study in which children, with identified difficulties in developing literacy skills, experienced different forms of interventions. One group of children were withdrawn and experienced general language activities - for example, they were taught how to classify pictures into sets - animals, fruit etc. Another group were exposed to words that rhymed and they were taught how to sort these into sets. A third group of children experienced the oral activities with rhyme but then used plastic letters to make the words. The teacher asked the child to make a regular word (e.g. "cat"). Once they had made that word they were asked to make a rhyming word (e.g. "mat"). Initially many children made the new word by using 3 new letters. The teachers continued to ask for more words from the same family until the child realised that all they had to do was to change the first letter. Bryant and Bradley considered that it was important that the child made this discovery for themselves and that they were not shown by the teacher. The children in this group achieved far better reading skills than the children in the other groups. All the children were followed up some years later and the children in the group who had had the experience of building words and recognising the analogy were still better readers than the children in the other groups.

This study clearly indicates that children need the opportunity to build words with letters using their sense of analogy. This activity is vital in consolidating the children's phonological experience and knowledge. Children should have opportunities to build words using plastic letters in the classroom.

After this experience with plastic letters other activities can be used to reinforce the children's sense of analogy.

● Give children different rimes and ask them to find as many words in each family as they can. Choose rimes that have the greatest utility; those that can generate the most words, for example -in, -on, -it, -at, -ake, etc. Gradually introduce words that have more complex letter strings but which form significant word families (ike, ight etc.)

● When children want to spell words for their own writing encourage them to think of words that they might know that are in the same family and to segment the word (or syllables) into onset and rime.

USING PHONEMES

With a firm knowledge of rimes and onsets the children will be able to read and spell many of the words that they require but they will need to develop a more sophisticated appreciation of the phonemes. There are two important skills that the children will have to develop - phonemic segmentation, splitting words and syllables into the constituent phonemes, (for example hat = h-a-t and shot = sh-o-t) and phonemic blending, blending individual phonemes to make syllables and words, (for example w-i-n = win and ch-i-p = chip)

When fluent readers encounter unfamiliar words they tend to break them into syllables; this makes the task of decoding the word more manageable - imagine trying to break the word "ilepidodendroid" into individual phonemes and then reconstituting them! Using syllables is a far more effective approach. Because of this, use small words or syllables with the children when investigating phonemes.

Segmentation

● Say short words and ask the children to tap out the number of phonemes in the word. They can represent the phonemes by putting down a corresponding number of counters.

● Ask the children to identify which phonemes they can hear in certain words. Say a word ('tap', for example). Start by asking the children how many sounds they can hear in the word. Let them tap out the number or put down the correct numbers of counters. Once you are sure that they are identifying the correct number and that they fully understand the task, ask then to tell you the individual sounds t-a-p.

● Encourage the children to use this technique when they are spelling words that they want to use in their writing. Check that they are able to break words into syllables when they are attempting multi-syllabic words and that they then try to identify the phonemes within the syllables.

Blending

- This, obviously, should be introduced as an oral activity. Take the opportunity to use the "incidental" times in the class just before lunch or break times or after a story to practise the skill with the children. Say the individual phonemes of a word clearly (e.g. w-i-n) and ask the children to tell you which word they make when you put them together.

- It is possible to make short tapes with constituent phonemes of words on. Ask the children to listen to the phonemes and write down the words that they make.

- Provide the children with individual plastic letters. Ask them to make as many words as they can. Talk to the children about the words that they have made; focus on the phonemes to allow the children to justify their spellings.

ASSESSMENT

Assessment has a central role in any successful teaching approach. It allows teachers to plan, to differentiate according to individual pupil's needs and to identify children who may be encountering difficulties. As Layton and Deeny (1995) correctly point out children who have seemingly fluent expressive and receptive language skills may have difficulties appreciating the phonological qualities in words.

The assessment techniques described below are generally criterion referenced (looking at skills that the children have) or ones that rely on teacher observation. They give indications of the next teaching steps.

Listening Skills

Assessing the children's listening skills may be achieved through careful teacher observation. The questions you may wish to ask include;

- can they accurately repeat a short passage of speech?

- how many elements of an instruction can they follow? ("Go to the office (1) get the register (2) and give it to Mrs Gibbons" (3))

- can the child distinguish between similar sounding words/letters?

If a child is causing you particular concern you may wish to assess their auditory short term memory. Ask the child to repeat a string of numbers after you. Start with 2 digits and gradually build up the number of digits.

Gathercole and Baddeley (1989) devised a very interesting assessment which looks at children's ability to repeat nonsense words; for example "bannifer". This assessment taps aspects of the children's ability to discriminate phonological elements in words, their auditory short-term memory and their ability to make analogies ('the word sounds like......')

Nursery Rhymes

As already noted children's knowledge of nursery rhymes is an important indicator of their growing phonological awareness. Determining their knowledge can be simply achieved by asking them to repeat a favourite rhyme. Pay particular attention to whether they include the rhyming pairs of words (of course, many of the pairs in nursery rhyme are not proper rhymes!). As with other things, there are better errors than others - thus it is better to say "John and Jill, Went up the hill" than "Jack and Susan, Went up the hill".

Recognition of rhyme

Lynette Bradley (1984) devised an oddity task to assess whether children can detect rhyme. Four words are read to the child (e.g. sun, bun, fan, gun) and the child has to identify which word is the odd one out. When this was tried with reception aged children in Suffolk they found it a very difficult task. It was not clear whether this was because they did not understand the concept of odd one out, if it put strains of their short term auditory memory (remembering 4 words) or because they couldn't identify the rhyme.

Because of the difficulties teachers and advisory staff devised a matching task in which the children were presented with cards with 4 pictures on and then given a card which rhymed with one of the four pictures. They were asked to put the card on top of the one with which it rhymed. This assessment proved far more accessible to the children but still identified the children who found rhyming difficult. This assessment may be carried out informally in the classroom with a suitable collection of rhyming pictures or objects.

Recognition of Alliteration

This, too, can be assessed through careful teacher observation. The Suffolk staff devised a complimentary matching task (as the previous one described for the recognition of rhyme) to determine if children could recognise words that began with the same sound.

Knowledge of Letter Sounds

Many schools have prepared sheets of randomly ordered letters to use when checking the children's knowledge of letter sounds. It is important to assess whether the children can recognise letter sounds and also generate them. Remember to include capital letters as well as lower case letters. (The sheets can also be used to assess children's knowledge of letter names.)

CONCLUSION

The approach that has been described in this book is based on some of the most current research into how children acquire reading skills. Children need to be able to recognise words by sight and they will be drawing upon the breadth of their language knowledge to make sense of what they are reading but they also need the skills which will enable them to read unfamiliar words - ways of understanding the significance of the alphabetical code. This latter skill is also fundamental for becoming an accurate and confident speller.

In the past many teachers, including myself, have approached this by concentrating, almost exclusively, on the individual sounds within the words (the phonemes). This approach does not recognise the underlying concepts and skills that the children need before they can find this a useful technique. These underlying competences relate to the children's general listening skills and the accuracy with which they can detect pattern, rhythm, similarities and differences within and between words. The children need to develop a phonological awareness which they can relate to print.

The activities described in the book are ones that are used successfully in classrooms. They are part of the rich language environment which is a feature of effective primary practice. They build on the children's existing knowledge and previous experiences and can be presented in a meaningful and enjoyable way. The activities also draw upon the literary tradition of rhyme and poetry which broadens the children's literary experiences.

By carefully assessing the pupils' understanding and skills it is possible to provide a structured and developmental approach for promoting accurate and functional knowledge of the letter-sound relationships which underpin fluent reading. It is also very enjoyable to teach!

Acknowledgement

Many of the ideas presented in the book have been drawn together by teachers and LEA support staff in Suffolk, particularly the work of the teachers in the Lowestoft, Bungay and Stradbroke schools.

REFERENCES

Adams, M.J. (1990) Beginning to Read: Learning and thinking about print. Cambridge, MA: MIT Press

Bradley, L (1984) Assessing Children's Reading Difficulties: A Diagnostic and Remedial Approach, 2nd Ed London, Macmillan Education

Bryant P.E. and Bradley, L. (1985) Children's Reading Difficulties. Oxford, Blackwell

Gathercole, S.E, and Baddeley, A.D. (1989) Evaluation of the role of phonological STM in the development of vocabulary in children: a longitudinal study . Journal of Memory and Language, **28,** 200 -213

Goswami, U. (1994) Reading by Analogy. In Reading Development and Dyslexia, eds Hulme, C. and Snowling, M. . London, Whurr Publishers Ltd

Goswami U. and Bryant, P.E. (1990) Phonological Skills and Learning to Read. London, Lawrence Erlbaum Associates

Layton, L. and Deeny, K. (1995) Tackling Literacy Difficulties. Can teacher training meet the challenge? British Journal of Special Education, 22, 1, 20 -23

Opie, I. and P. (1969) Children's Games in Street and Playground. Oxford University Press.